INSIGHTS

EARTH, AIR, AND ATOMS

ROBIN KERROD

INSIGHTS

EARTH, AIR, AND ATOMS

ROBIN KERROD

Oxford University Press

A QUARTO BOOK

Published by
Oxford University Press, Walton Street, Oxford OX2 6DP

Oxford New York Toronto Delhi Bombay Calcutta Madras Karachi Kuala Lumpur
Singapore Hong Kong Tokyo Nairobi Dar es Salaam Cape Town Melbourne Auckland Madrid
and associate companies in Berlin Ibadan

Oxford is a trade mark of Oxford University Press

A CIP catalogue record for this book is available from the British Library.

ISBN 0 19 910058 6

This book was designed and produced by
Quarto Children's Books Ltd
The Old Brewery 6 Blundell Street London N7 9BH

Art Director Nick Buzzard
Managing Editor Christine Hatt

Editor Elizabeth Spiers
Designer Trish Going
Illustrators Evi Antoniou, Janos Marffy, Paul Richardson,
Guy Smith (Mainline Design), Keith Ward
Picture Researcher Liz Eddison
Picture Manager Dipika Parmar-Jenkins

The Publishers would like to thank the following for their help in the preparation of this book: Karen Ball, Stephen Pople.

Picture Acknowledgements
Quarto Publishing would like to thank the following for supplying photographs and for permission to reproduce
copyright material. While every effort has been made to trace and acknowledge all copyright holders, we would
like to apologize should any omissions have been made.

AEA Technology, page 23br. Australian Overseas Information Service London, pages 10c, 11b, 33b. Nick Buzzard,
page 25b. Colorific, pages 16a (inside flap), 19ar, 26cr, 37bc. Eye Ubiquitous / Trip, pages 15ar, 15br, 29bl, 49cl, 50cl,
51ar. Andrew Gasson / Trip, page 31ar. Robin Kerrod, pages 12b, 16ar, 24br, 24ar, 26ar, 35ar, 36bl, 42br, 42cr, 47cl.
Edna Palian, pages 14ar, 27c, 36ar. Quarto Publishing Plc, page 34cr. Christopher Rennie / Trip, pages 40al, 48br
(inside flap). Rover Group, page 46cl. Helene Rogers / Trip pages 25a, 30c, 31cl, 40cr, 44br. Scipix, pages 35c, 47ar.
Spacecharts, pages 11r, 12c, 13al. Sony UK Limited, page 42ar. Telegraph Colour Library UK, pages 10b, 11al, 14b, 17b,
19al, 19br, 24b, 28c, 28br, 33ar, 33cr, 36br, 37br, 38br, 39br, 43bl, 45 (inside flap), 46ar, 49ar, 50b, 51cr. US Naval
Observatory, page 13ar (inside flap). Joan Wakeline / Trip, pages 41c, 41ar. Tony Waltham, page 37c. Wildlife Matters, page 18a.

Key: a = above, b = below, l = left, r = right, c = centre

Front jacket photographs supplied by: Eye Ubiquitous / Trip – centre, Telegraph Colour
Library UK – above right. Back jacket photograph supplied by: AEA Technology.

Typeset by Central Southern Typesetters, Eastbourne, East Sussex
Manufactured in Hong Kong by Regent Publishing Services Ltd
Printed in Singapore by Star Standard Industries (Pte) Ltd

CONTENTS

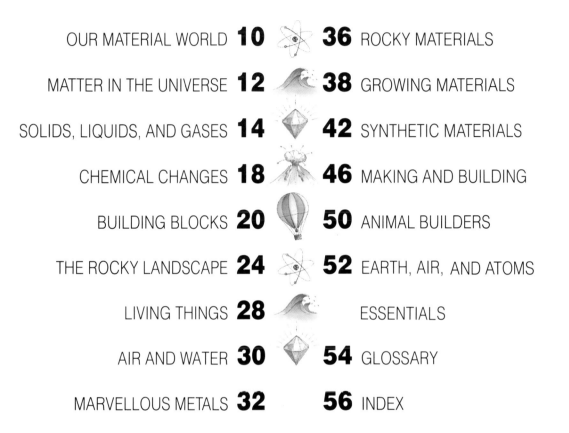

OUR MATERIAL WORLD

A million or more years ago in Africa, our early ancestors began picking up stones to make tools. Later, they fitted wooden handles to the stones to make better tools, such as axes and hammers. They were starting to use the natural materials around them to improve their way of life. Today, we use huge amounts of different materials to produce the things that make our lives easier, more comfortable, and more enjoyable. But most of them are artificial materials, not natural ones.

▼ Woolly wanderers
Vast flocks of sheep graze the open range in Australia, the leading wool-producing country in the world. The sheep are rounded up several times a year for dipping, shearing, and lambing.

Some of the most common materials we use are steel, plastics, and paper. These materials do not occur in nature. But we do use natural materials to make them, and we call these raw materials. They may be mineral, vegetable, or animal.

Most of our raw materials come from the ground. For example, we extract iron from a type of mineral called an ore (see pages 32–33). We take minerals from the ground by mining. We make many plastics from liquid petroleum (crude oil), which we take from the ground by drilling.

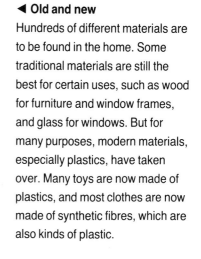

◄ Old and new
Hundreds of different materials are to be found in the home. Some traditional materials are still the best for certain uses, such as wood for furniture and window frames, and glass for windows. But for many purposes, modern materials, especially plastics, have taken over. Many toys are now made of plastics, and most clothes are now made of synthetic fibres, which are also kinds of plastic.

◀ **Log jam**
Logs floating in a 'log pond' at a saw-mill, waiting to be cut into sawn timber. Wood has been one of our most useful materials since prehistoric times. Today, it is used not only for building construction, but also for making pulp and paper.

Many valuable raw materials come from plants and animals. For example, we make paper from wood, which we get from trees. Sheep provide us with wool for making cloth.

Minerals, petroleum, wood, and wool are some of our most useful raw materials. We get others from the sea, and even from the air we breathe!

Many of the products we use are made by treating raw materials with chemicals. Some, such as plastics, are made entirely from chemicals. We call these materials synthetics.

▶ **Classic car**
Metals, in particular iron and steel, are the main materials used in a car. The very heavy engine block is usually made of cast iron, and the body from steel sheet. Copper is used for the electrical wiring and lead in the battery.

▶ **Rust-red landscape**
An open-cast mine in western Australia producing iron ore, one of our most valuable raw materials. The ore is rust-red, which explains the colour of the landscape. Australia is one of the world's largest iron ore producers, with an output of over 110 million tonnes (121 million tons) a year.

MATTER IN THE UNIVERSE

The Earth we live on, and that provides all our raw materials, is just a tiny speck in the Universe. The Universe contains everything, and is made up of stuff called matter, travelling through space. Most matter is gas, found in the billions of stars that are scattered about the Universe. Only here and there do we find lumps of denser matter like the Earth.

▼ Ringed splendour
The beautiful ringed planet Saturn, with six of the moons that circle around it. Saturn is made up mainly of gas, while the moons are a mixture of rock and ice.

The Earth is a ball of rock that moves in space around the Sun. It is one of nine bodies that we call planets. Some of the other planets are rocky and others are made up mainly of gas. The gassy ones, such as Jupiter, are giants compared with the Earth.

The planets form the main part of the Sun's family, or Solar System. Many of the planets also have smaller bodies called moons circling around them. The Earth has one, the Moon. Swarms of mini-planets (asteroids), icy lumps (comets), and rocky particles (meteoroids) also whizz around our Solar System.

Many rocky pieces shower down on the Earth all the time. We can sometimes see them burn up in the atmosphere, as the fiery streaks we call meteors, or shooting stars.

Galaxies of stars

The night sky is full of stars. From the Earth they seem tiny, but in fact they are very big. They are great balls of hot gas like the Sun. They appear tiny only because they are so very far away. The brightest star in the sky is Sirius. It is one of the closest stars. Yet it still lies 90 million million kilometres (56 million million miles) away!

The stars in the Universe are not dotted about everywhere in space. They are gathered together in

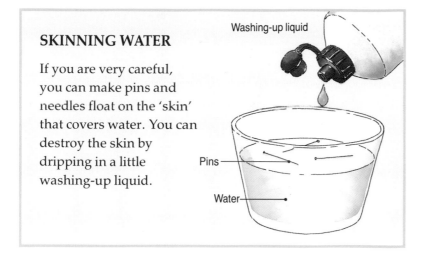

SKINNING WATER

If you are very careful, you can make pins and needles float on the 'skin' that covers water. You can destroy the skin by dripping in a little washing-up liquid.

Washing-up liquid

Pins

Water

◄ **Pond skater**
This little bug can be seen walking about on the surface of ponds. If you look closely, you can see how its feet make 'dents' in the water. This shows that water seems to be covered with a kind of skin.

▼ **Balloon fiesta**
Burners below the open ends of hot-air balloons heat up the air inside. This becomes lighter than the air outside and so rises.

shape of any container it is put in. You can change its shape easily by applying pressure to it. Water also flows from a higher level to a lower level. Anything that flows is called a fluid.

Air is a mixture of gases. Like all gases, it has no definite size or shape. It takes the size and shape of any container it is put in. Its size as well as its shape can be changed by applying pressure. Like water, air can flow – it is a fluid.

Crystals, skins, and drag

Most matter on the Earth is found in the solid state. It can be living or dead (organic), or something that has never lived (inorganic). Rocks are inorganic materials. Many rocks are made up of a mixture of tiny, glassy pieces. They are crystals of the different minerals that make up the rock.

Liquids seem to be covered with a kind of skin. This is caused by forces at the surface pulling downwards, and is called surface tension. This 'skin' allows some insects to walk on water.

Like most gases, air is invisible and so light that we hardly know it is there. But we can feel it when it moves, for example, when the wind blows. Air presses on us with a pressure called the

▼ Fertile fields

This mountain is a dormant (sleeping) volcano, which has erupted many times in the past. Very hot molten rock from deep underground poured out and flowed down the mountainside. There it cooled and turned solid. The action of the weather broke down the volcanic rock and helped to turn it into rich soil. Farmers try to cultivate as much of the mountainside as possible. To do this, they build flat terraces, which are much easier to work than sloping land.

▲ Speedy shape

Grand Prix racing cars are streamlined to reduce air resistance (drag). This helps them to reach speeds of 300 km/h (200 mph).

atmospheric pressure. It also pushes against anything moving. We call this air resistance 'drag'.

Changing states

On a very cold day, a puddle of water freezes into ice. On a hot day, we see steam rise from a puddle, which gradually disappears. As the temperature changes, the water changes its state. It changes from liquid to solid when it is cooled, and from liquid to gas (steam) when it is heated. Many substances, even rocks and air, will change their state if their temperature changes enough.

As the temperature rises, many solid substances will eventually melt and become liquid. A liquid will eventually boil, turning rapidly into a gas. As the temperature falls, the opposite happens. A gas will condense, turning into a liquid, and a liquid will freeze, becoming a solid.

For each substance, melting (and freezing) and boiling (and condensing) take place at fixed temperatures. These are called the melting and boiling points.

KINETIC THEORY

The kinetic theory explains the differences between the three states of matter. It states that all matter is made up of moving particles.

Solid state

In solids, the particles are so tightly bound to one another that they can only vibrate. In liquids, the particles can move about, but they still attract one another. In gases, the particles are far apart and can move about freely.

Liquid state

Solids change into liquids, and liquids into gases, when their particles gain more kinetic energy (for example, by being heated), and are able to move apart from one another.

Gaseous state

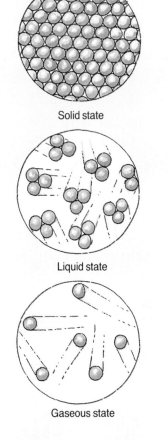

◄ **Misty mystery**
Misty effects, for example at pop concerts, are made using dry ice. The ice sublimes, that is turns directly into gas without passing through a liquid stage.

CHEMICAL CHANGES

The matter in our world is constantly changing. Liquid water changes into ice when it freezes and into steam when it boils. But water does not change into a different substance when it freezes or boils. Freezing and boiling are called physical changes. Water, ice, and steam are three different forms of the same substance. But many substances change completely. When a candle burns, the wax disappears. You cannot get it back no matter what you do. Completely new substances have been formed. This type of change is called a chemical change.

All matter is made up of substances we call chemicals. Chemistry is the science that studies the nature and properties of all substances. Every chemical is made up of basic 'building blocks' called elements (see pages 20–23).

Candle wax belongs to the group of chemicals called hydrocarbons, because they are made up of hydrogen and carbon only. When the wax burns, it reacts with oxygen in the air. The hydrogen in the wax combines (links up) with oxygen to form a new chemical, hydrogen oxide. We know this better as water. The carbon combines with oxygen to form another new chemical, carbon dioxide.

◀ **Burning questions**
Burning is a chemical reaction that gives out energy in a number of ways. For example, it gives out energy as heat, which we can feel. It also gives out light energy, in the form of flames.

THE ACID TEST

Acids and alkalis are two of the commonest kinds of chemical. Scientists can tell whether a solution contains acid or alkali by testing it with litmus paper. Red litmus paper stays red in an acid, but turns blue in an alkali. Blue litmus paper stays blue in an alkali, but turns red in an acid. We call litmus an indicator, because by changing colour it indicates whether something is acidic or alkaline.

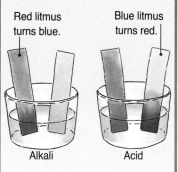

Red litmus turns blue.   Blue litmus turns red.

Alkali   Acid

QUICK, QUICK, SLOW

When left out in the wet, steel drums gradually become covered with a film of rust (left). Rusting is a slow reaction. When fireworks explode (right), their chemicals burn rapidly in a fast reaction, which gives out energy as light, heat, and sound.

▲ Checking the changes
Chemistry students at work in a laboratory. They carry out experiments to study the changes that take place when chemicals react together.

▶ Puffed out
A collie after exercising. It gains the energy to run about by 'burning' food inside its body.

Burning gives out energy as light and heat. Water and carbon dioxide are both gases at the temperature of burning and disappear into the air.

Breathing and rusting

Burning is an example of one of the commonest chemical reactions, called oxidation. In oxidation, oxygen combines with other substances. Other oxidation reactions occur all around us.

Oxidation takes place when we breathe. We take in oxygen through our lungs to 'burn' the food we eat. This burning process produces the energy we need to grow and move. Iron 'burns' too if it is left out in damp air. It combines very slowly with oxygen in the air to form rust.

SOUR, SOOTHING, AND SALTY

A lemon, an antacid medicine, and a salt cellar each contain a different class of chemical. The lemon contains sour-tasting citric acid. The medicine contains soothing milk of magnesia, an alkali that fights too much acid in the stomach. The salt cellar contains salty sodium chloride. Acids and alkalis form salts when they react together.

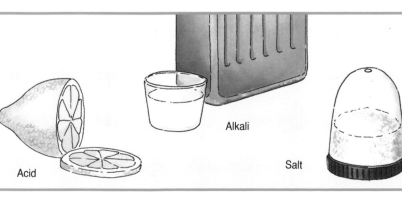

Acid

Alkali

Salt

BUILDING BLOCKS

There are millions of different chemicals in the world about us and inside our own bodies. But they are made up of only about 90 substances, called the chemical elements. The elements are the 'building blocks' of all the matter in the Universe. Each element is made up of tiny particles we call atoms. The atoms are made up of even tinier particles.

Most of the elements are solid substances at normal temperatures. There are a few gases, and only two liquids. The solid elements are mostly metals, such as gold and iron. Carbon and sulphur are two of the non-metals. Oxygen and nitrogen are two of the gases (also non-metals). The two liquids are mercury (a metal) and bromine (a non-metal). Mercury is unique because it is the only liquid metal.

The elements are all different from each other. In particular, they differ in the way they combine with other elements. Scientists say that they have different chemical properties. But some elements have quite similar properties, and can be grouped together in families.

A table of elements

Chemists have drawn up a table that shows these family relationships. They call it the periodic table. A version of the table is shown on the right. The rows of elements going across the table are called periods. The columns of elements going down are called groups. The elements in the groups have similar chemical properties. The most reactive elements, which will combine readily with other

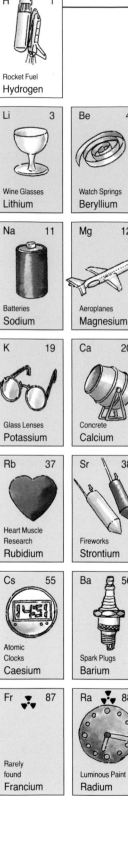

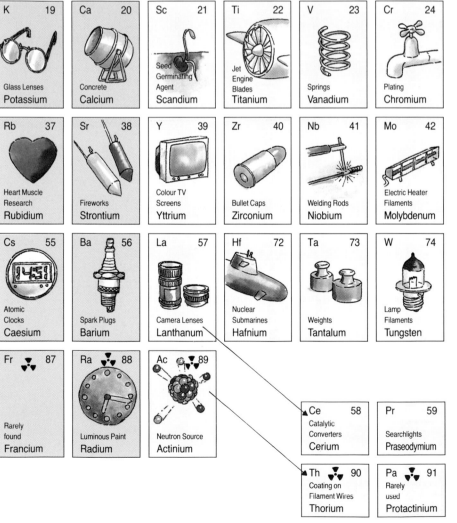

▼ Arranging the elements
This is a modern version of the periodic table, a method of arranging the chemical elements first drawn up in 1869. The person who devised it was a Russian chemist, Dmitri Mendeleyev.

The table is divided up into vertical groups and horizontal periods. The elements in the groups have similar chemical properties. The properties of the elements in the periods change gradually from left to right.

The elements appear in the table in the order of their atomic number, that is the number of protons they contain (see pages 22–23). This number is shown (top right) in each box in the table. The box also includes the chemical symbol (top left) of the element. The pictures indicate one use of the element. (A further six chemical elements, atomic numbers 104–109, have been made by scientists in the laboratory, but only in minute quantities.)

KEY

- Light metals
- Heavy metals
- Semi-metals
- Non-metals
- ★ Artificial elements
- ☢ Radioactive elements

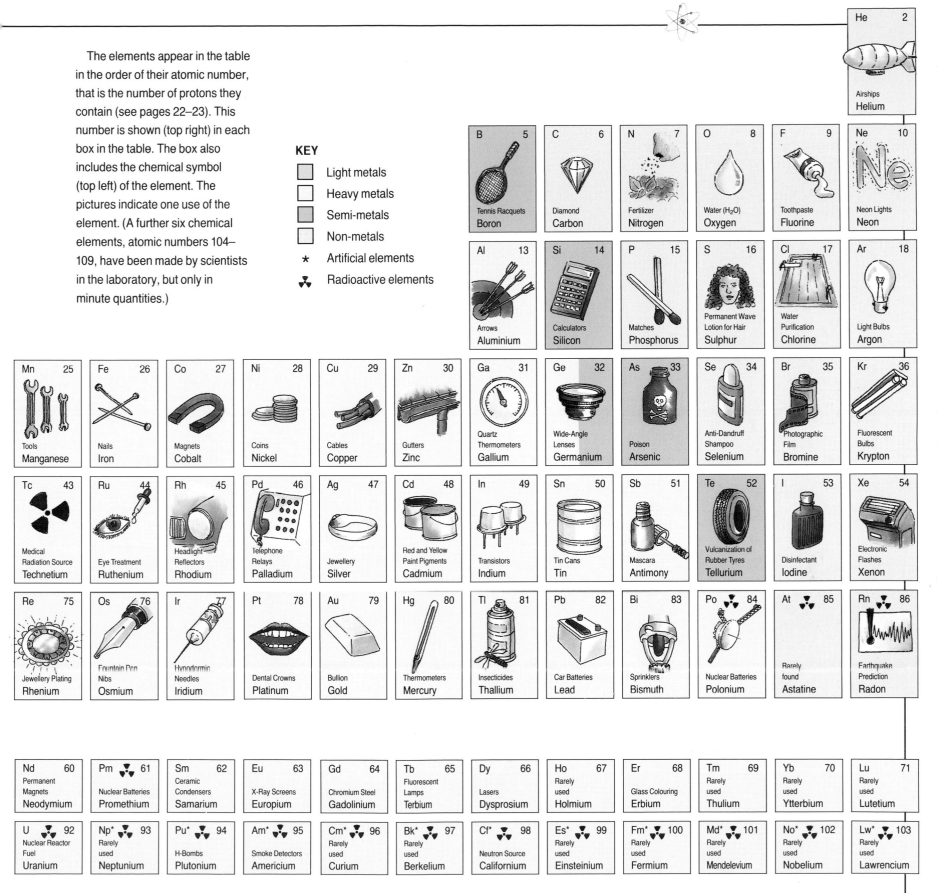

He 2 — Airships — Helium					
B 5 — Tennis Racquets — Boron	**C** 6 — Diamond — Carbon	**N** 7 — Fertilizer — Nitrogen	**O** 8 — Water (H_2O) — Oxygen	**F** 9 — Toothpaste — Fluorine	**Ne** 10 — Neon Lights — Neon
Al 13 — Arrows — Aluminium	**Si** 14 — Calculators — Silicon	**P** 15 — Matches — Phosphorus	**S** 16 — Permanent Wave Lotion for Hair — Sulphur	**Cl** 17 — Water Purification — Chlorine	**Ar** 18 — Light Bulbs — Argon

Mn 25 — Tools — Manganese	**Fe** 26 — Nails — Iron	**Co** 27 — Magnets — Cobalt	**Ni** 28 — Coins — Nickel	**Cu** 29 — Cables — Copper	**Zn** 30 — Gutters — Zinc	**Ga** 31 — Quartz Thermometers — Gallium	**Ge** 32 — Wide-Angle Lenses — Germanium	**As** 33 — Poison — Arsenic	**Se** 34 — Anti-Dandruff Shampoo — Selenium	**Br** 35 — Photographic Film — Bromine	**Kr** 36 — Fluorescent Bulbs — Krypton
Tc 43 — Medical Radiation Source — Technetium	**Ru** 44 — Eye Treatment — Ruthenium	**Rh** 45 — Headlight Reflectors — Rhodium	**Pd** 46 — Telephone Relays — Palladium	**Ag** 47 — Jewellery — Silver	**Cd** 48 — Red and Yellow Paint Pigments — Cadmium	**In** 49 — Transistors — Indium	**Sn** 50 — Tin Cans — Tin	**Sb** 51 — Mascara — Antimony	**Te** 52 — Vulcanization of Rubber Tyres — Tellurium	**I** 53 — Disinfectant — Iodine	**Xe** 54 — Electronic Flashes — Xenon
Re 75 — Jewellery Plating — Rhenium	**Os** 76 — Fountain Pen Nibs — Osmium	**Ir** 77 — Hypodermic Needles — Iridium	**Pt** 78 — Dental Crowns — Platinum	**Au** 79 — Bullion — Gold	**Hg** 80 — Thermometers — Mercury	**Tl** 81 — Insecticides — Thallium	**Pb** 82 — Car Batteries — Lead	**Bi** 83 — Sprinklers — Bismuth	**Po** ☢ 84 — Nuclear Batteries — Polonium	**At** ☢ 85 — Rarely found — Astatine	**Rn** ☢ 86 — Earthquake Prediction — Radon

Nd 60 — Permanent Magnets — Neodymium	**Pm** ☢ 61 — Nuclear Batteries — Promethium	**Sm** 62 — Ceramic Condensers — Samarium	**Eu** 63 — X-Ray Screens — Europium	**Gd** 64 — Chromium Steel — Gadolinium	**Tb** 65 — Fluorescent Lamps — Terbium	**Dy** 66 — Lasers — Dysprosium	**Ho** 67 — Rarely used — Holmium	**Er** 68 — Glass Colouring — Erbium	**Tm** 69 — Rarely used — Thulium	**Yb** 70 — Rarely used — Ytterbium	**Lu** 71 — Rarely used — Lutetium
U ☢ 92 — Nuclear Reactor Fuel — Uranium	**Np*** ☢ 93 — Rarely used — Neptunium	**Pu*** ☢ 94 — H-Bombs — Plutonium	**Am*** ☢ 95 — Smoke Detectors — Americium	**Cm*** ☢ 96 — Rarely used — Curium	**Bk*** ☢ 97 — Rarely used — Berkelium	**Cf*** ☢ 98 — Neutron Source — Californium	**Es*** ☢ 99 — Rarely used — Einsteinium	**Fm*** ☢ 100 — Rarely used — Fermium	**Md*** ☢ 101 — Rarely used — Mendelevium	**No*** ☢ 102 — Rarely used — Nobelium	**Lw*** ☢ 103 — Rarely used — Lawrencium

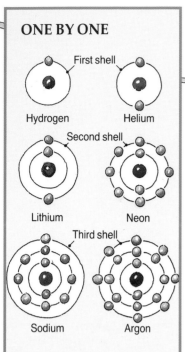

First shell

Hydrogen   Helium

Second shell

Lithium   Neon

Third shell

Sodium   Argon

Every chemical element has a different number of protons in the nucleus, and of electrons moving around the nucleus. There are the same number of electrons as there are protons. The number of protons is called the atomic number.

The electrons in an atom are arranged in shells. Hydrogen is the simplest atom, with a single electron. Helium comes next with two electrons, which fill the first shell. Lithium follows, with a third electron in a second shell. The other elements are built up in a similar way, with electrons being added one by one, and shell by shell.

elements, are those in the first group (hydrogen, lithium, etc) and those in the last group but one (fluorine, chlorine, etc).

Gamma rays

Atoms beyond number

Carbon is a common element, found for example in pencil 'lead'. If you could chop up a piece of pencil lead into smaller and smaller pieces, you would eventually come to the smallest pieces that can exist. These are the carbon atoms. They are tinier than you could possibly imagine. The tip of your pencil contains billions of them!

The other elements are made up of atoms in a similar way. All the atoms in one element are similar to each other. But the atoms of every element are different from the atoms of every other element.

▼ **Picturing the atom**
In an atom, a number of tiny electrons move around a central nucleus. They are found at different distances from the nucleus in layers called shells. Each shell can hold a certain number of electrons. The arrangement of the electrons into shells is called the electronic structure of the atom.

Electron

Nucleus

Shell

DECAYING ATOMS

Radioactive nucleus

Beta rays

Alpha rays

The atoms of most elements always stay the same. But the atoms of some elements are unstable. From time to time, their atoms give off particles and radiation.

These elements are radioactive. Uranium and radium are examples.

Radioactive elements give off three kinds of radiation, called alpha, beta, and gamma. Alpha and beta rays are streams of tiny particles, while gamma rays are a form of electromagnetic radiation.

Inside the atom

The word atom comes from a Greek word meaning 'that which cannot be divided'. This is not really a good name because scientists can now split atoms and detect the particles they contain. The atoms of different elements are all made up of the same kinds of particle. But they each contain different numbers of these particles.

At the centre of every atom is a nucleus. This contains two main kinds of particle. They are called protons and neutrons. Circling around the nucleus are several much tinier particles called electrons. The protons have a positive electric charge. The electrons have a negative electric charge. Electrons and protons attract one another, because of their opposite charges. This electrical attraction holds the atom together.

Protons, neutrons, and electrons are the main subatomic ('smaller than the atom') particles. But scientists know of more than 200 subatomic particles altogether. They all have a different mass or electric charge. Some of these play a part in keeping the atom together. Scientists now believe that many particles are made up of even tinier particles called quarks.

▼ **Deadly glow**

A beautiful blue glow lights up this 'radiation pond', in which radioactive materials are stored. The water in the pond glows blue when particles given out by the radioactive materials pass through it at high speed.

▲ **Smashing events**

When high-speed atomic particles collide, other kinds of particle are produced. These particles leave tracks in a detecting chamber (above). Scientists carry out such collisions to investigate the structure of matter.

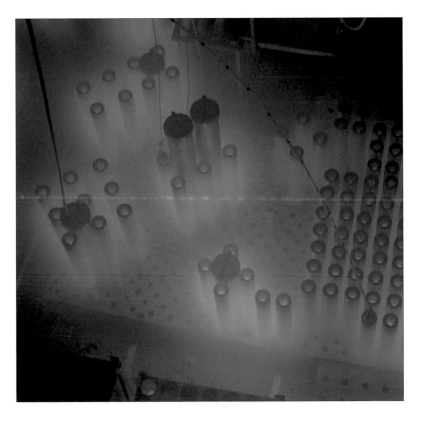

THE ROCKY LANDSCAPE

The Earth is made up mainly of many kinds of rock. Some rocks are born in the fiery heart of volcanoes. Others are formed from broken-down pieces of more ancient rocks and even fossils. The surface rocks are always being attacked by wind and waves, rain and sun, ice and frost. In time, these weathering forces reduce even the hardest rocks to handfuls of dust, and totally alter the landscape. Other changes are brought about by movements of the surface, which cause earthquakes and make mountains.

▲ Crystal shapes
In some rocks, minerals form well-shaped crystals. The blue crystal here is tourmaline.

Only the rocks in the Earth's outer layer, the crust, are hard and rigid. The crust is quite thin (up to 40 kilometres [25 miles]) compared with the size of the Earth (12,756 kilometres [7926 miles] across).

The rocks beneath the crust are much softer, and are able to flow. They are very hot, and under great pressure. In some places the crust is weak, and the soft, hot rocks force themselves up towards the surface. As they push upwards, the rocks melt. This molten rock is called magma.

◀ Wrinkling rock
Lava flowing from Kilauea, one of Hawaii's most active volcanoes. The surface is cooling in the air, and forming a stiff, wrinkled crust. But underneath the crust, the lava is still molten and flowing.

▼ Cold cinders
When lava has fully cooled, it forms a rock like this – a jumbled mass of cinder-like material.

▶ Geode jewels

Ordinary-looking stones can sometimes reveal a hidden beauty. Some are hollow, and if you crack them open carefully, you may find that they are lined with crystals. This type of stone is called a geode, or vug. Mostly, the crystals inside are quartz, which is the commonest of all minerals.

Fire-formed rocks

Sometimes the magma gets right to the surface and spurts out into the air. This is what happens when a volcano erupts. The magma flows out as lava but quickly cools to form solid rock, such as basalt. Sometimes the rising magma gets trapped below the surface and cools more slowly, forming the rock called granite.

Basalt and granite are examples of igneous, or fire-formed, rocks. Basalt has tiny crystals because it cools so quickly that they do not have time to grow. In granite, the crystals are much larger.

Layered rocks

The weather causes rocks at the surface of the Earth gradually to wear away and break up into smaller and smaller pieces. In time, layers of these pieces, called sediments, build up and are changed by heat and pressure into solid rock. This is called sedimentary rock. Sandstone, which is made up of compressed grains of sand, is a typical example of a sedimentary rock.

Other sedimentary rocks formed when ancient seas dried up and deposited the chemicals they

▼ Cutting the Canyon

The Grand Canyon in the western USA is one of the natural wonders of the world. The Colorado River has cut through the rocks over millions of years, exposing hundreds of different layers.

LAYERS OF TIME

In some places on Earth, layers of sedimentary rock have built up, one on top of the other. The top layers are usually younger than the bottom layers, so we can think of the layers of rock as 'layers of time'.

Scientists have named the different time periods in which particular kinds of rock were laid down. They use these names when describing the Earth's history.

Quaternary Period 0–2 million years ago

Tertiary Period
2–65 million years ago

Cretaceous Period
65–144 million years ago

Jurassic Period
144–213 million years ago

Triassic Period 213–248 million years ago

Permian Period 248–286 million years ago

Carboniferous Period
286–360 million years ago

Devonian Period 360–408 million years ago

Silurian Period 408–438 million years ago

Ordovician Period 438–505 million years ago

Cambrian Period
505–590 million years ago

Precambrian Period

contained. Limestone is an example of this type of rock. Some seas left behind piles of skeletons of tiny creatures. This became the white rock called chalk.

Drifting continents

The soft rocks underneath the crust slowly wander across the Earth. They take sections of the crust with them. Geologists, the scientists who study the Earth, call these sections 'plates'.

The continents 'ride' on plates and are carried along by them, slowly and in different directions. This movement is called continental drift. Europe and America are slowly moving apart because of continental drift. And the Atlantic Ocean is widening by a few centimetres every year.

Earthquakes, volcanoes, and mountains

The moving plates are always rubbing and pushing against one another. Often they get stuck, then suddenly give way. This makes the ground shake, causing earthquakes.

▲ Black beach
We think of beaches as golden, but they are not in Hawaii! Some of the beaches there are black, made up of volcanic sand.

▼ White cliffs
Chalk cliffs run along part of the southern coast of England. Most chalk beds were laid down during the Cretaceous Period.

BUILDING MOUNTAINS

The movement of the Earth's plates can cause mountains to form. When two plates moving in opposite directions collide, one plate rides up over the other. The result is that the surface rocks

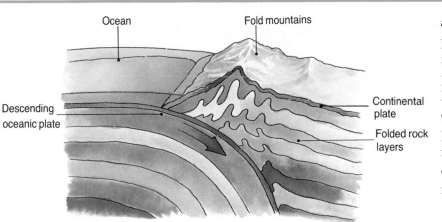

Ocean
Fold mountains
Descending oceanic plate
Continental plate
Folded rock layers

are compressed and pushed upwards, forming fold mountains. The picture shows this happening at the edge of a continent. The oceanic plate underneath the sea is sliding beneath the continental plate, forcing it upwards.

Rubbing between plates also causes heat by friction (rubbing). This melts some of the rock, which often forces its way up to the surface to create volcanoes. When plates meet head-on, one plate rides up over the other, wrinkling the surface and making mountain ranges. This is happening, for example, along the western coast of South America. The result is the great mountain range of the Andes.

▲ Changed rock
A piece of slate, a hard rock that splits into flaky layers. It is a metamorphic, or changed rock, formed from the soft rock shale.

▼ Soil structure
Soil is made up of mineral, vegetable, and animal materials. The basic material is mineral, and consists of fine, rocky particles.

This is mixed with organic materials, such as rotted plants, animal wastes, and household rubbish. Plant roots and burrowing animals improve the soil texture.

LIVING THINGS

A huge variety of living things is found on Earth, from bacteria you can see only under a microscope to gigantic creatures like the blue whale, which grows up to 33 metres (108 feet) long. There are millions of different species (kinds) of plants and animals. Insects alone account for more than one million species!

The science of living things is called biology. Its two main branches are botany, the study of plants, and zoology, the study of animals.

Although all species of living things are different, they do have certain things in common. First, they need food to give them energy to grow and move. Plants make their own food by a process called photosynthesis. But animals must get their food by eating plants or other animals that eat plants.

Second, living things must take in oxygen from the air to 'burn' their food to provide energy (see pages 18–19). This process is called respiration.

Third, living things must be able to reproduce. This means producing new members of the species, called offspring. Non-living things are not able to reproduce. Usually, reproduction is sexual. This means male and female parts must come together to produce offspring.

The living cell

The bodies of plants and animals are made up of basic units called cells. Cells group together to form tissues and organs. Animal and plant cells are similar in several ways. They are made up mainly of a jelly-like substance called cytoplasm, held within a membrane (a skin). Plants have rigid cell walls, made of a woody material called cellulose.

▼ At the waterhole
The plains of eastern and southern Africa are home to the biggest herds of wildlife on Earth. In the dry season, the scattered waterholes attract a great variety of animals.

PIGS AND PLANTS

Pigs reproduce sexually. The male produces sex cells called sperms, which he introduces into the female when they mate. The sperms combine with (fertilize) the female's sex cells, the eggs. The fertilized eggs grow into

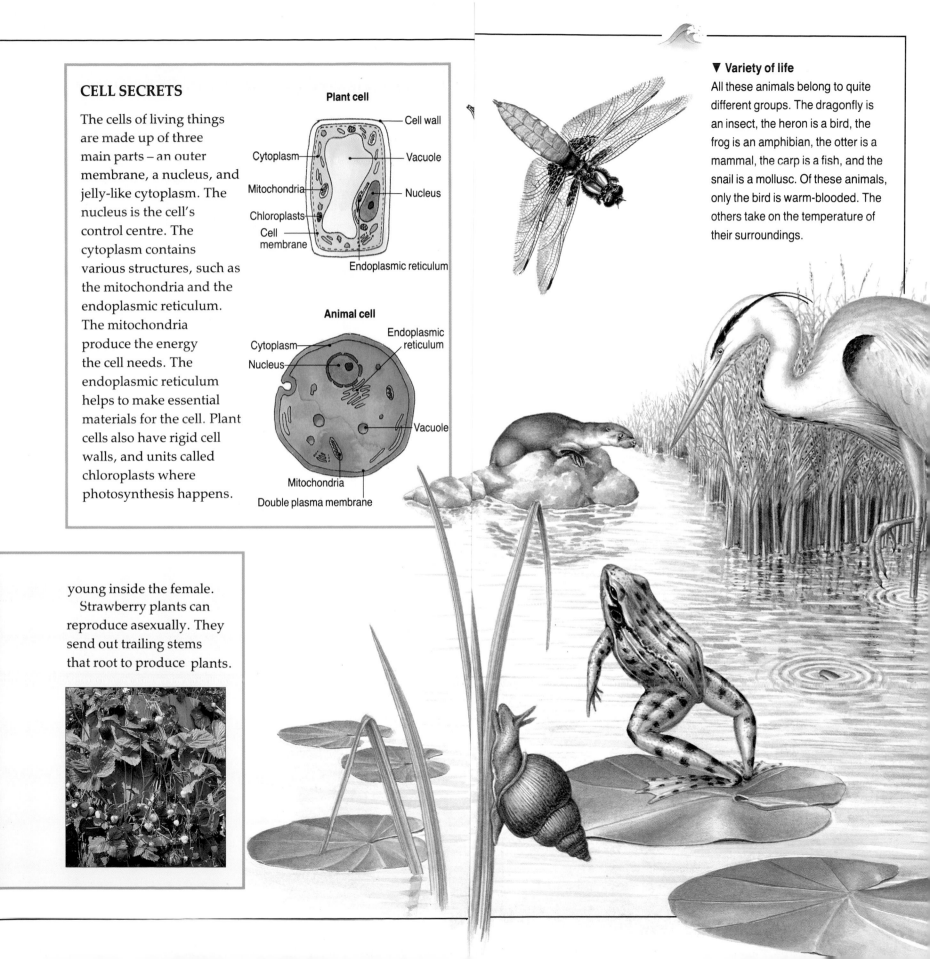

CELL SECRETS

The cells of living things are made up of three main parts – an outer membrane, a nucleus, and jelly-like cytoplasm. The nucleus is the cell's control centre. The cytoplasm contains various structures, such as the mitochondria and the endoplasmic reticulum. The mitochondria produce the energy the cell needs. The endoplasmic reticulum helps to make essential materials for the cell. Plant cells also have rigid cell walls, and units called chloroplasts where photosynthesis happens.

Plant cell

- Cell wall
- Cytoplasm
- Vacuole
- Mitochondria
- Nucleus
- Chloroplasts
- Cell membrane
- Endoplasmic reticulum

Animal cell

- Cytoplasm
- Endoplasmic reticulum
- Nucleus
- Vacuole
- Mitochondria
- Double plasma membrane

young inside the female. Strawberry plants can reproduce asexually. They send out trailing stems that root to produce plants.

▼ Variety of life

All these animals belong to quite different groups. The dragonfly is an insect, the heron is a bird, the frog is an amphibian, the otter is a mammal, the carp is a fish, and the snail is a mollusc. Of these animals, only the bird is warm-blooded. The others take on the temperature of their surroundings.

AIR AND WATER

For living things, air and water are the most important substances on Earth. Living things must take in oxygen from the air in the atmosphere to stay alive. They must also take in water regularly because it is the substance that transports food and chemicals between the living cells in their bodies. In the world about us, water is exchanged between the atmosphere and the land. This is one of the main things that affects our weather.

The vital gas in the air that living things must breathe is oxygen. About one-fifth of the air is oxygen – nearly four-fifths is nitrogen. There are also traces of other gases, including argon and carbon dioxide.

Nitrogen and argon are very inert. This means that they do not react with other chemicals easily. Carbon dioxide is the gas animals give out as a waste product when they breathe. Plants take in carbon dioxide to help make their food.

Carbon dioxide is also formed when fuels burn. So much of this gas is being produced by cars and factories that it is gradually turning the atmosphere into a kind of greenhouse. This is starting to warm our climate and disrupt our weather.

Water, water everywhere

Water covers seven-tenths of the Earth's surface. Most of it is found in the great oceans, like the Pacific and the Atlantic, which are on average about 4 kilometres (2.5 miles) deep. This water is very

THE WATER

This would, perhaps, be a better name for our planet than 'The Earth'! This is because watery oceans cover over twice the area of the rocky continents. More water is found as ice at the North and South Poles.

◄ Salt lake
Some lakes are very salty. When water evaporates from them, the salt is deposited. It is often collected for commercial use.

THE WATER CYCLE

Every day, millions of tonnes of water evaporate from the Earth's surface into the air. On average, the same amount of water returns to the surface from the air as rain and snow. This endless water cycle is one of the most important processes in nature, and has a great effect on our weather.

Most water vapour evaporates into the air from the oceans. But large amounts are also given off by trees and other plants, in a process called transpiration.

► Penguin paradise

Adélie penguins on the Antarctic ice. The ice sheet covering this vast, cold wilderness is 1,600 m (1 mile) thick in places.

◄ Moist monsoon

Here, in India, the seasonal summer wind, called the monsoon, blows on to the land from the sea. It is full of moisture and brings heavy, warm rain.

salty because it contains dissolved chemicals, mostly sodium chloride (common salt). Fresh water is found in rivers and lakes, and frozen water forms the great ice sheets that cover the North and South Poles. Only about one per cent of the Earth's water is fit for us to drink!

Water is disappearing from the surface of the Earth all the time. It is being evaporated (turned into vapour, or gas) by the heat of the Sun. In the atmosphere, the vapour cools and condenses into water droplets. We see them as clouds in the sky. When the droplets get big and heavy enough, they fall from the clouds as rain. This exchange of water between land and air is part of a never-ending water cycle.

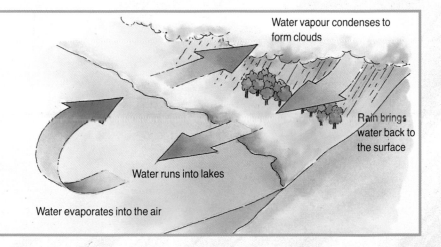

Water vapour condenses to form clouds

Rain brings water back to the surface

Water runs into lakes

Water evaporates into the air

The use of metals has changed through history. About 5,000 years ago, humans began using bronze, and this period is called the Bronze Age. About 3,000 years ago, the Iron Age began. For the past 150 years, we have lived in the Steel Age. Thanks to the strength of steel, we can build long bridges and tall skyscrapers.

MARVELLOUS METALS

Metals are probably the most important materials we use on Earth. Without them, we could not build engines and machines or giant structures like skyscrapers. We would be without electricity, because our electricity generators and circuits all need metal wires to carry electric current. We use more iron than all the other metals put together. Aluminium, copper, nickel, tin, and lead are also produced in large quantities. Like iron, they are extracted from minerals mined from the ground and processed in fiery furnaces.

Most of the chemical elements are metals (see pages 20–23). But only a few of them can be found`as metal in the ground. These are called native metals, and include gold and silver. They are found in metal form because they do not react easily with other chemical elements. Gold found in the tombs of Ancient Egyptians looks as bright and attractive today as it did 4,000 years ago.

Most metals are much more reactive. They can only be found in minerals, where they are combined with other elements. Minerals that can be used to produce metals are called ores.

Ore deposits are scattered throughout the Earth's crust. Some are found on or near the surface, where they can be extracted by open-cast mining. Iron ores and bauxite (aluminium ore) are often mined in this way. Other ores are found deeper down and are extracted from underground mines.

Fierce furnaces

Most metals are extracted from their ores by smelting (roasting) them at high temperatures in furnaces. For example, iron is made by smelting

▲ Any old iron
A scrapyard in Germany. Every year we recycle (use again) large quantities of iron and steel scrap in steelmaking furnaces. This saves both materials and energy.

▲ Solid gold
Bars of pure gold. In everyday use, gold is always found in the form of an alloy (mixture) with copper or silver. This makes it much more hard-wearing.

◄ Gold mine
The Mount Morgan gold mine in Queensland, Australia. This country is now a major gold producer, with an output of over 250 tonnes (275 tons) a year.

MAKING STEEL

The iron produced in a blast furnace is not pure enough to be useful, so it has to be purified. We call the purified metal steel.

Most steel today is produced by the basic-oxygen process. The impurities in the iron are burned out by a high-speed jet of oxygen. The process takes place in a tiltable furnace called a converter.

The best steel is made from selected steel scrap in electric furnaces. In electric refining, the scrap is just re-melted. Other metals may be added, according to the steel-making 'recipe'.

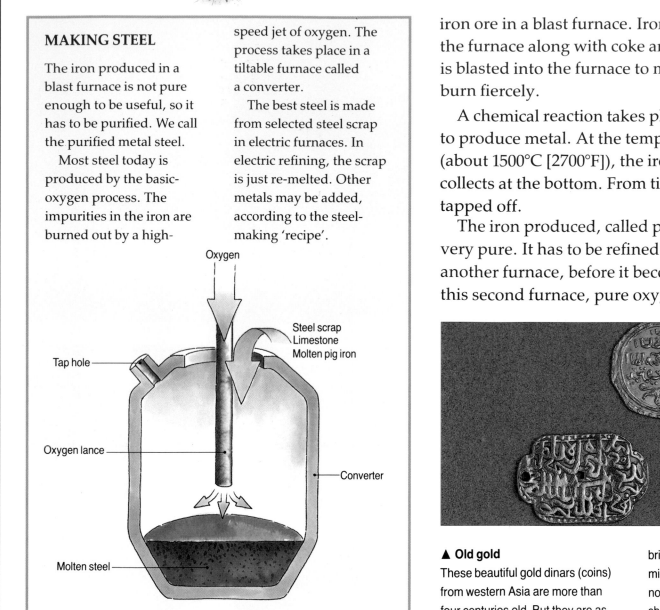

Oxygen

Tap hole

Steel scrap
Limestone
Molten pig iron

Oxygen lance

Converter

Molten steel

iron ore in a blast furnace. Iron ore is heated in the furnace along with coke and limestone. Air is blasted into the furnace to make the coke burn fiercely.

A chemical reaction takes place inside the furnace to produce metal. At the temperature of the furnace (about 1500°C [2700°F]), the iron is molten, and it collects at the bottom. From time to time, it is tapped off.

The iron produced, called pig iron, is still not very pure. It has to be refined (purified) further in another furnace, before it becomes really useful. In this second furnace, pure oxygen is blasted through

▲ Old gold
These beautiful gold dinars (coins) from western Asia are more than four centuries old. But they are as bright today as when they were just minted. This is because gold does not react with any ordinary chemical elements.

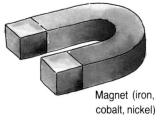

Magnet (iron, cobalt, nickel)

Cutting tools (steel, chromium, tungsten)

◄► Metals galore
All these different objects are made from different mixtures of metals. The purpose of mixing metals is to create alloys with better properties.

For example, mixing chromium and nickel with steel makes stainless steel, which does not rust. Steel can be made very hard by adding chromium and tungsten.

Jewellery (gold, silver, platinum, copper)

Cutlery (stainless steel: steel, chromium, nickel)

the molten pig iron. It burns out most of the impurities. The metal that results is iron containing a little carbon. We know it better as steel.

All kinds of alloy

Steel is an example of an alloy. An alloy is a metal mixture. Most of the metals that we use are alloys. Our copper-coloured coins are made of the alloy bronze, which is a mixture of copper and tin. Our silver-coloured coins are made of the alloy cupronickel (copper and nickel). Brass (copper and zinc) and stainless steel (iron, nickel, and chromium) are two other familiar alloys.

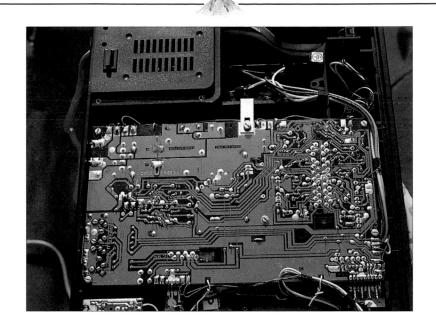

▲ Soldered circuits
The underside of an electronic circuit board for a radio. The blobs of solder join wires from the various components (on the other side of the board) to the copper circuits 'printed' on the board. Solder is a tin/lead alloy that melts at a low temperature.

◄ Light construction
Building the European Airbus in Toulouse, France. Like all planes, it is built of aluminium alloys, which are light but strong.

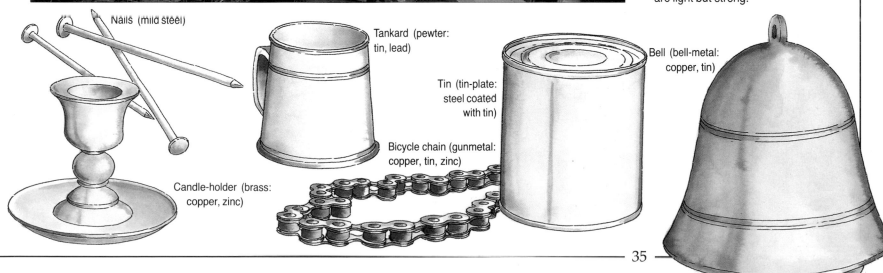

Nails (mild steel)

Tankard (pewter: tin, lead)

Bell (bell-metal: copper, tin)

Tin (tin-plate: steel coated with tin)

Candle-holder (brass: copper, zinc)

Bicycle chain (gunmetal: copper, tin, zinc)

ROCKY MATERIALS

The metal ores are not the only useful minerals in the Earth's crust. We use many others, from talc, the softest mineral, to diamond, the hardest. We can use talc (for talcum powder) and diamond (for gems) in much the same state as we take them from the ground. But we process many other minerals into quite different products.

▲ **Great glaze**
This pottery bowl was made attractive by painting and glazing.

Sand is one of the commonest materials in the Earth's crust. It is a finely divided form of the mineral quartz, which is silicon dioxide. It is used to make glass and silicon chips.

Clay is also a very common mineral. It is useful because it can be baked into pottery, bricks, and tiles. These products are called ceramics. Cement is another ceramic product, made from a mixture of clay, iron ore, and limestone. When cement is mixed with sand, gravel, and water, it becomes our most useful building material – concrete.

We also use large quantities of rock for building work. Most is crushed and added to concrete, or used for road foundations. But some is carefully

◄ **Glass houses**
Glass-walled tower blocks in the centre of Los Angeles, USA. Glass, which is made mainly from sand and limestone, has been used in buildings for about 500 years.

▼ **Sandy chips**
Pure sand is also the starting point for the miracle product of the age – the silicon chip.

MOHS SCALE

Some minerals look so alike that it is difficult to tell them apart. However their hardness may vary considerably.

Mineralogists rate hardness on the Mohs hardness scale, which is named after the German who devised it, Friedrich Mohs. On this scale, talc is 1, fluorite is 4, quartz is 7, and diamond is 10. No natural substance is harder than diamond.

Talc
1

Fluorite
4

Quartz
7

Diamond
10

cut and used as building stone in tower blocks, bridges, and tunnels.

Sparkling gems

Rare minerals like diamond have quite a different use. Diamond looks like a dull piece of glass when it is mined. But when expertly cut, it sparkles and flashes all the colours of the rainbow. It is the most prized of the precious stones we call gems, which have been in great demand as jewellery for thousands of years.

Other gems are ruby (red), sapphire (blue), and emerald (green). Like diamond, these gems need careful cutting for their beauty to be revealed.

▲ Rock fibres
This rock, made up of a mass of fibres, is known as asbestos. It is a silicate rock called chrysotile. Fabrics made from the fibres are used widely in fireproof suits and safety curtains.

▶ Dazzling diamond
The many facets of this superbly cut diamond reflect a rainbow of colours. A diamond may be cut with more than 50 facets to bring out its full beauty.

▼ Diamonds for industry
The white crystals embedded in this mineral specimen are industrial diamonds known as bort.

GROWING MATERIALS

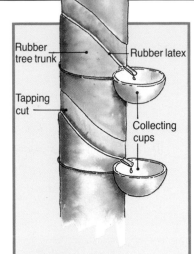

T he living world provides us with many valuable materials for use in the home and in industry. Trees are our greatest living resource. They provide us with timber (wood). We use the wood for building work and for making paper, plastics, and textile fibres. Fibres are also widely produced on farms, from both plants and animals. The advantage of using living resources for materials is that we have a constant supply. In contrast, the mineral resources we mine are limited and bound to run out one day.

Thousands of years ago, great forests covered most of the land areas of the Earth. But when our ancestors became farmers, they began clearing away the trees and tilling the soil to grow crops. The process is still going on. Large areas of natural forest remain only in northern Europe, North America, and tropical regions near the Equator.

In the northern forests, most trees are evergreen

SUPERSAP

Rubber is a naturally elastic material obtained from the latex (sap) of rubber trees. Workers collect the latex in cups, after tapping (cutting) the trees. Workers get crude rubber from the latex by treating it with acid. Most rubber is now synthetic.

▼ World forests

The main forest regions of the world are today found in the far north and around the Equator. In both regions, the main trees are evergreen. They not only provide us with timber, but also provide many kinds of wildlife with shelter.

▼ Cork talk

Bark newly stripped from cork oak trees, which are found widely in the Mediterranean region. The bark is softened by boiling before being shipped to users.

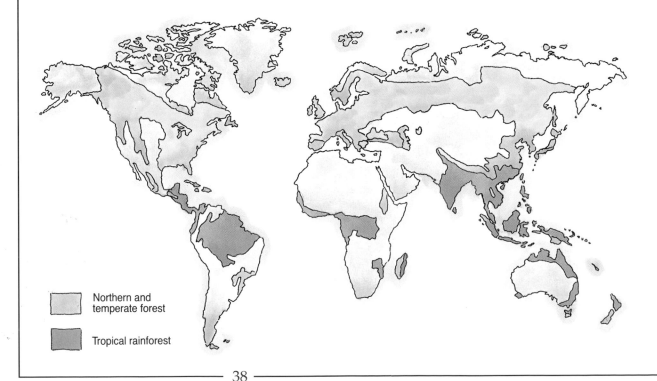

Northern and temperate forest

Tropical rainforest

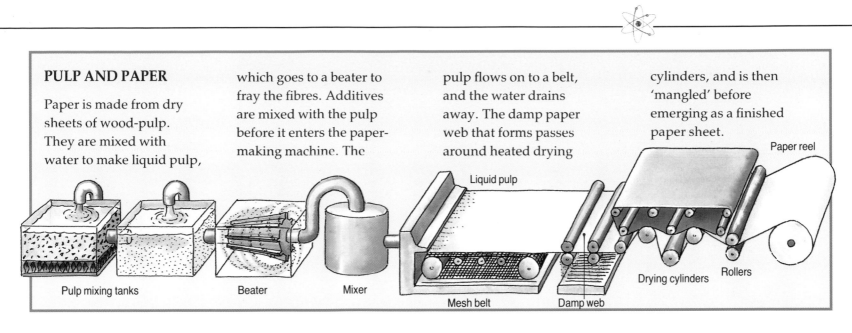

PULP AND PAPER

Paper is made from dry sheets of wood-pulp. They are mixed with water to make liquid pulp, which goes to a beater to fray the fibres. Additives are mixed with the pulp before it enters the paper-making machine. The pulp flows on to a belt, and the water drains away. The damp paper web that forms passes around heated drying cylinders, and is then 'mangled' before emerging as a finished paper sheet.

Pulp mixing tanks

Beater

Mixer

Liquid pulp

Mesh belt

Damp web

Drying cylinders

Rollers

Paper reel

conifers, such as pine and spruce. They bear their seeds in cones, and have thin leaves like needles. Needle-like leaves do not lose heat as quickly as broad leaves, and help to protect the trees from the bitter winter cold. Foresters plant this kind of tree in managed plantations elsewhere because it is fast-growing.

The trees in the tropical rainforests are also evergreen, but they have broad leaves. They include species such as teak and mahogany. Too much of the world's rainforest is now being cut down, particularly in South America and South-East Asia, putting thousands of species of animals and plants in danger. Loss of the trees and their roots also causes enormous amounts of soil to be washed away. This is called soil erosion.

Hardwoods and softwoods

Tropical trees like teak are known as hardwoods, because their wood is hard and wears well. Much of it is made into furniture. Conifer trees give much softer timber and are known as softwoods. They are used mainly in building construction and for making wood pulp. This is the starting point for

▼ Pulp plant
Logs to be processed at a pulp mill. Newsprint, the paper used for newspapers, is made from wood-pulp produced by shredding wood with a grindstone. Paper for books and magazines is made of pulp from chemically treated wood.

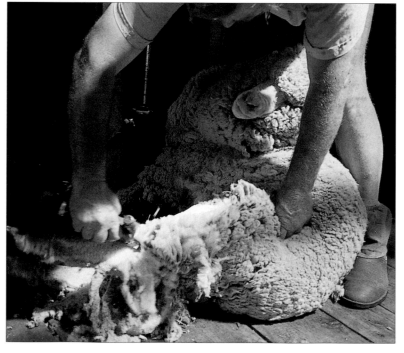

THROWING SILK

Silk is the most prized of all textile materials. Its long, fine threads are soft and shiny. We get them from the cocoon spun by the silkworm. This 'worm' is actually the caterpillar of a cream-coloured moth

◀ **Cuddly camels**
Up in the Andes mountains of South America, llamas (left) and alpacas are raised for their soft woolly fleece. They belong to the same family as the camel, whose hair is also used as a textile fibre.

making paper, and cellulose plastics (such as celluloid) and fibres (such as rayon).

Farm fibres

People started spinning and weaving fibres to make cloth many thousands of years ago. The first fibre they used was wool, from the curly fleece of wild sheep. Later, they began to farm sheep.

Sheep provide most of our wool today. Special breeds of sheep are raised, the most important being the merino. This animal can produce a fleece weighing more than 10 kilograms (22 pounds). Other valuable animal fibres are obtained from cashmere and angora goats, certain members of the camel family, and even from a caterpillar – the industrious silkworm.

The main plant farmed for fibre is cotton, which grows best in hot, moist subtropical regions. The fibres form around the cotton seed in the seed boll

▲ **Fast fleece**
Shearing sheep in New South Wales, Australia. Shearers use electrical clippers rather like the ones that barbers use. The most skilful can work unbelievably fast. The record is over 800 lambs sheared during a nine-hour day!

that feeds on mulberry leaves. The process of gathering the silken threads from cocoons into yarn is called throwing.

Silkworm

Cocoon spun by silkworm

◄► Picking cotton

A harvester at work in the cotton fields in Mississippi, USA (right). The machine uses revolving spindles to strip the fluffy cotton bolls (left) from the plants. The USA is the world's top cotton producer.

(case). Flax is a fibre crop widely grown in cooler regions. Its fibres are called linen. They come from the stalks of the plant, which grows like wheat.

Seeds and oil

Cotton and flax plants also give another valuable product – oil. Cottonseed oil is used instead of fats in 'healthy' foods, such as low-fat margarines. We get linseed oil from flax seeds. It is widely used in paints and varnishes.

Many other plants are also grown on a large scale for the oil that can be extracted from their seeds. Many farms now grow rape, which has brilliant yellow flowers and a strong scent. Some buses now use biodiesel, a fuel made from rapeseed oil. Sunflowers, olives, and soya beans are other oil-producing crops.

▼ Oily flowers

Sunflowers are a popular garden plant, but they are now also farmed widely as a crop. They are grown for their seeds, which give an oil that is used for cooking and for making low-fat spreads.

SYNTHETIC MATERIALS

Plastics have now become as important as metals and wood, but they are made from chemicals, not from natural raw materials. They are synthetic (artificial) materials. We use many other synthetics too. We wear shoes with synthetic leather uppers and synthetic rubber soles. We put on synthetic-fibre clothes, coloured by synthetic dyes and washed with synthetic detergents. We make many of these synthetic products from chemicals in petroleum, called petrochemicals. In many ways, petroleum is more valuable as a source of chemicals than it is as a fuel.

▲ Mouldy plastic
A children's clock radio, moulded in plastic. It is colourful, tough, and easy to keep clean.

Petroleum (crude oil) is a thick, greenish-black liquid that bubbles up from underground wells. This 'black gold' is a mixture of hundreds of different chemicals called hydrocarbons. It becomes really useful only when these hydrocarbons are separated into various parts called fractions.

This is done by heating the oil, and then allowing its vapour to cool at different temperatures in a tall column (a fractionator). The oil splits up into liquid fuels such as petrol and kerosene, thicker oils, and gases. The thicker oils and gases can then be processed further to produce a wide variety of

▲ Oil crackers
In these towers at an oil refinery, thick oil is cracked (broken down) to produce useful petrochemicals.

▼ Pretty poly
Colourful plastic sheeting has hundreds of uses. This plastic is PVC (polyvinyl chloride).

PLASTIC CHAINS

Plastics are materials that are easy to mould. That is because their molecules, or basic particles, are very long. They are made up of long chains of carbon atoms.

— Hydrogen atoms

— Carbon atoms

▼ If you could see a bit of a polythene molecule, it might look like this. On the same scale, the whole molecule would stretch for more than 1000 metres (3300 feet)! Only carbon atoms can form long chains like this.

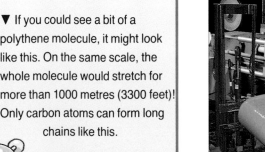

GREASE LOVERS

The synthetic detergents we use for washing have molecules with two different ends. One end is grease-loving, the other water-loving. The grease-loving ends attach themselves to greasy dirt. The water-loving ends are attracted to the washing water, which carries the dirt away.

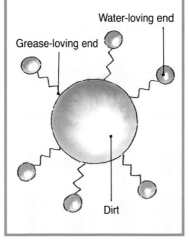

Water-loving end

Grease-loving end

Dirt

petrochemicals. These are the starting point for many common plastics and other synthetics.

Plastic polys

Polythene, polyvinyl chloride (PVC), and polystyrene are three of our best-known plastics. Polythene is used to make bowls and bags. PVC is used to make pipes and artificial leather. Polystyrene is used to make clear containers and foam tiles for use on ceilings.

You will notice that the names of these plastics all start with 'poly-'. That is because chemists call plastics polymers, a word meaning 'many parts'. This refers to the way they are made, or synthesized.

Plastics are unlike most ordinary chemical substances because their particles, or molecules, are very long. This is what gives plastics their special properties and makes them easy to shape.

◄ Tight rope
A 'skywalker', clad in warm and waterproof plastic clothing, hauls himself up an ice cliff on a plastic rope. Most ropes used for skywalking and mountaineering are made of nylon, which is very much stronger than ordinary rope and does not rot.

► High flier
Like most modern toys, this kite is made largely of plastic. Light, but strong, plastic rods make up the frame, while the fabric is made of synthetic fibres.

MAKING AND BUILDING

All the materials we have looked at so far – minerals, metals, wood, and plastics – have to be made into the products we buy. Most products are now manufactured in factories. The word manufacture means 'making by hand', and until about 200 years ago, most products were made by hand, in the home. Then machines were invented to do most of the work. It became much easier and quicker to make products in large quantities. This caused the Industrial Revolution. Today, most products are made by machine.

▲ Moulding metals
Molten metal being cast into moulds at a steel foundry. This process has been used for shaping metals for over 5,000 years. The moulds may be made of special firm sand, or of metal. Sand moulds can be used only once. Metal moulds can be used again and again. Casting in metal moulds is often called die-casting.

Most machines are made of metal. One of the oldest methods of making metal products is casting. This means pouring molten metal into a mould of the shape you want. When the metal cools, it takes the shape of the mould, just like a jelly does when it sets. For example, the engine blocks of cars are made by casting.

Forging is another common method, in which hot metal is hammered into shape. This is the method blacksmiths use to shape horseshoes and iron gates. Sometimes the hot metal is forged by gradually squeezing it. This is done on huge hydraulic presses, which work by liquid pressure.

RISE OF THE ROBOTS

Robots are taking over! This is headline news in many industries today. In the car industry, for example, robots work alongside humans on the production line. They carry out jobs like spraying paint and welding, which are unpleasant for humans to do. But these robots are not human-like. They are simply very flexible mechanical arms.

ASSEMBLY LINE

Most cars are now built on an assembly line. Henry Ford in the USA introduced the moving assembly line in 1913. Workers stand beside a moving conveyor carrying part of the car, and add components to it.

These pictures show some of the stages in car assembly.

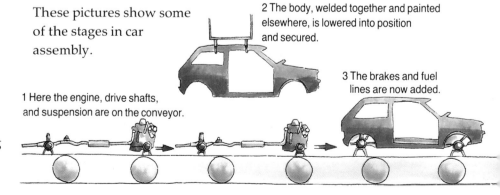

2 The body, welded together and painted elsewhere, is lowered into position and secured.

3 The brakes and fuel lines are now added.

1 Here the engine, drive shafts, and suspension are on the conveyor.

Presses also shape cold metal sheet, which is used to make car bodies, for example. Sheet is made by rolling red-hot slabs of metal in a series of rolling mills. These are long, heavy cylinders that turn, squeezing the metal flat between them.

Drilling and cutting

After a piece of metal has been shaped by one of these methods, it is usually finished off by drilling, cutting or grinding.

These operations are carried out by machines called machine tools. They have powerful motors and tools with hard cutting edges to cut through metal. Drills and lathes are two of the commonest machine tools. A lathe is used to turn a piece of metal while other tools cut it to the correct size.

Bolting and welding

Metal parts often have to be joined together (assembled) to make a finished product. This may be done simply by using nuts and bolts. A car engine is assembled in this way.

Metal parts can be joined together more strongly by welding. For example, car bodies are made by welding. A welder uses an electric or gas 'torch' to heat the edges of the pieces to be joined. Then the

▲▶ Big squeeze
Using thousands of tonnes of pressure, a huge hydraulic (liquid-pressure) press slowly squeezes a red-hot steel ingot into shape (above). When it is cool, machine tools will cut it and grind it (right) to exactly the right size.

4 The seats and wheels are brought in on other conveyors and fitted.

5 The bonnet and the hatch door are fitted outside, pedals and gears inside.

6 With the fitting of windows, doors, and bumpers, the car is nearly complete.

7 Final parts are added, and the car is ready for the road.

▼ Shifting steel
Cranes shift steel girders into position on a large building site. The girders form the rigid frame of the building.

welder adds molten metal to join the hot edges. When the metal cools, it forms a strong, permanent joint. Today, robots often do the welding.

Building big

In factories, engineers and workers make quite small products. But outside, they build enormous things, such as bridges, skyscrapers, and dams.

The engineers who do this kind of construction work are called civil engineers. The main materials they use are steel and concrete. Everything they build has a 'backbone' of steel rods or girders. Skyscrapers like the Sears Tower in Chicago, in the United States, which is 443 metres (1453 feet) high, could not be built without them.

The longest bridge in the world is the Humber Bridge in north-east England. It has a central span of 1410 metres (4626 feet). This type of bridge is called a suspension bridge, as the deck is suspended from steel cables that go over tall towers.

Most dams are massive. The Grand Coulee Dam in Washington State, in the United States, weighs a colossal 20 million tonnes (22 million tons). It relies on its enormous weight to hold back the water behind it, so is called a gravity dam.

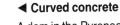

◄ Curved concrete
A dam in the Pyrenees in north-east Spain. It is an arch dam – its strength lies in its curved shape.

► Chunnelling
Work under way on the Channel tunnel, or 'Chunnel'. It runs 50 km (31 miles) from Cheriton, near Dover to Sargatte, near Calais.

HIGH RISE

One of the first building materials used was mud, but this is too weak for building high. Stone is stronger, but heavy. High stone towers can be built only if they are very thick at the base. Using iron, huge structures can be built. But the highest ones need a steel frame.

1 Mud hut

2 Leaning Tower of Pisa, Italy (completed 1350). Stone, 54.5 metres (179 feet).

3 Eiffel Tower, France (completed 1889). Iron, 300 metres (985 feet).

4 Empire State Building, New York (completed 1931). Steel frame, 381 metres (1250 feet).

5 CN Tower, Toronto, Canada (completed 1975). Steel frame, 555 metres (1822 feet).

ANIMAL BUILDERS

Human beings are not the only members of the animal kingdom that are clever at building. Animals weave, cement, drill, gnaw or dig to create homes to raise their young and shelter from their enemies. They use many kinds of material, such as grass, gossamer, mud, wood, and wax. Birds, bees, and beavers are among the many animal families that show extraordinary building skills.

Most birds build nests, some of them with great skill. House martins build their neat nests of mud pellets under the eaves of houses. Most small woodland birds, such as wrens, tits, and finches, build cosy cup-shaped or rounded nests lined with moss, feathers, hair, and spiders' webs.

The African weaver bird is one of the most skilful nest-builders. It uses its bill as a needle to thread long grasses into domed nests, often tying knots to keep the strands in place.

OVENBIRD'S NEST

A South American bird called the rufous hornero builds a rounded mud nest shaped like an old-fashioned baker's oven. This is why it is more commonly called the ovenbird. The nest has a narrow entrance, leading to a central chamber lined with grass.

▲ Tunnelling termites
This tall mound of earth was constructed by ant-like creatures called termites. They built it from earth that they dug out while tunnelling underground in search of food. Termite mounds may be more than 6 m (20 ft) tall. Inside, they are divided up into chambers. In the centre, the queen is imprisoned in a cell, where she lays thousands of eggs every day.

◄ The paper-makers
A wasp and its nest of six-sided cells. Bees build their nest cells of wax, whereas wasps build them of paper. They chew old pieces of wood or tough plant material to make a kind of wood-pulp, which they spit out to construct the interconnecting rows of cells. The wasps that build paper nests like this are called social wasps, because they live in colonies.

Silk and wax

There are weavers in the insect world too – weaver ants. These creatures build leafy nests with silk threads provided by their larvae (young). Some ants bend the leaves, while others squeeze the larvae, which makes them give out a sticky thread that binds the leaves together.

But of all insects, bees show the most building skill. Using wax they make in their bodies, they build an intricate structure made up of six-sided cells. This forms the honeycomb in which they store their honey and raise their young. Some kinds of wasp build a similar structure out of a paper-like material they make by chewing wood.

Animal engineers

Many animals make their homes by moving earth. There are all kinds of burrower, which dig out tunnels underground. They include rabbits, gophers, and moles. But the cleverest engineer of them all is the dam-building beaver.

▲ Sitting pretty
Young house martins peer inquisitively out of their well-made nest of mud and grass.

▶ Beavering away
A North American beaver, hard at work. This animal lives in streams in wooded areas of the northern USA and Canada.

BUSY BEAVERS

Beavers build their homes, or lodges, on the banks of streams or on islands that they make from mud and branches. For safety, they like the entrance to their lodge to be under water. If the water level is too low, they dam the stream with branches, mud, and stones. They build their 'living room' above the water line, with an air hole on top. Somewhere nearby under the water, the beavers store twigs and branches for their winter food.

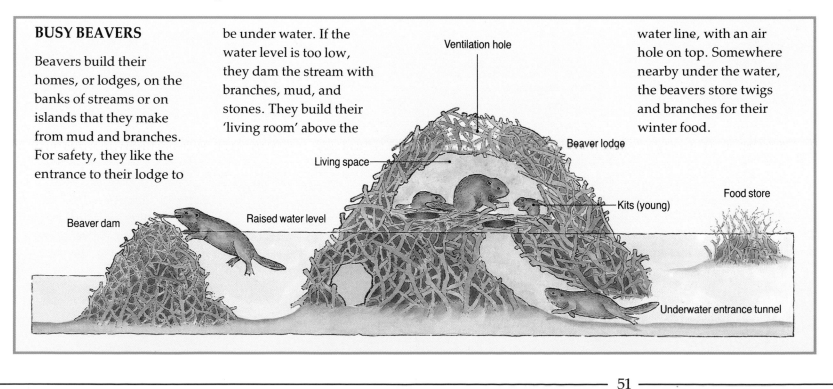

Ventilation hole

Beaver lodge

Living space

Food store

Beaver dam

Raised water level

Kits (young)

Underwater entrance tunnel

EARTH, AIR, AND ATOMS ESSENTIALS

Matter is the stuff that the Universe is made of. It can take the form of solid rocks, flowing liquids, or puffs of gas. By manipulating natural materials and the chemicals we make from them, we have created a fascinating variety of products, among them metals and magnets, dyes and drugs, paper and plastics. This fact-kit provides you with a summary of essential information about the kinds of material in our modern world.

1 What can the matter be?

This book is all about matter, which is the stuff that fills the Universe. The Universe means everything that exists – matter, energy and space.

2 Building blocks

Our world is full of millions upon millions of different substances of all shapes and sizes, from grains of sand less than a millimetre across to whales bigger than a house. But all these things are made up of only about 90 basic substances, which we call the chemical elements. Carbon and gold are examples of chemical elements.

3 Up and Atom

Every substance is made up of minute particles, so tiny that 100 million of them side by side would measure only 1 cm (0.4 inch)! These particles are called atoms. Each chemical element has a different kind of atom.

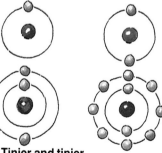

4 Tinier and tinier

The atoms themselves are made up of even tinier particles. The main ones are protons, neutrons, and electrons. The protons and neutrons are grouped together in the solid centre, or nucleus, of the atom. The much smaller electrons whizz round the nucleus.

5 States of matter

All the millions of substances on Earth are found in the form of a solid, a liquid, or a gas – the three states of matter.

6 Solids, liquids, and gases

A solid is usually hard and rigid, and has a fixed size and shape. A liquid has a definite size but no definite shape. It takes the shape of any container it is poured in. A gas has no fixed size or shape, and fills completely any container it is put in.

7 All change

Ice is a solid. But if you heat it, it melts into a liquid – water. If you heat water, it eventually turns into a gas – water vapour. By heating, you have made a solid and a liquid change their state. Most substances will change their state if you heat (or cool) them enough.

8 Big rocky lump

We live on a big lump of matter – the Earth. Much of the Earth is made up of solid rock. But more than two-thirds of the Earth's surface is covered with liquid – water. And there is a layer of gas – air – above the surface.

9 Fiery rocks

Many of the rocks in the Earth's hard outer layer, or crust, formed when molten rock from deep inside the Earth surged on to the surface from volcanoes and cooled. They are called igneous rocks. Other kinds of igneous rocks formed when molten rock cooled below the surface.

10 Layer upon layer

The other main kind of rock formed when layers of different materials built up and were pressed into a solid mass. They are called sedimentary rocks. In most sedimentary rocks the layers, or strata, are easily seen.

11 The changing landscape

The Earth's surface is always changing, usually slowly, but sometimes quickly. Volcanoes and

earthquakes bring about sudden changes. They are usually caused by movements of sections, or 'plates', of the Earth's crust.

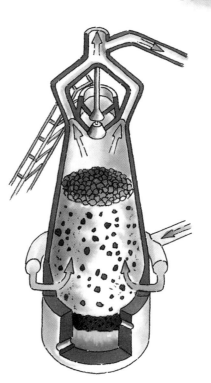

12 The living world

Rocks, water, and air make up the non-living, or inorganic, part of our world. You and other humans, dogs and cats, tulips and trees, and all plants and animals make up the other part of the world – the living, or organic part.

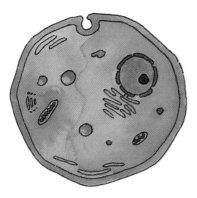

13 Science in cells

All living things are made up of tiny units called cells. Some simple plants and animals consist of only one cell. But advanced animals are made up of billions. Inside the cells of living things, processes take place that enable them to live, grow, and reproduce.

14 Materials in the raw

For many thousands of years, human beings have used the materials around them – both living and non-living – to make things and build things. Before we start processing them, we call them raw materials.

15 Wood from the trees

One of the oldest materials used, wood, is still one of the most important. It is used not only as solid timber, but also as pulp to make paper and chemicals.

16 Fibres for fabrics

Cloth was one of the first man-made materials, and spinning and weaving cloth were among the first crafts human beings practised. Wool from sheep, and cotton from plants have always been the most widely used fibres for making cloth.

17 Rocks and minerals

The most useful raw materials are the rocks and minerals we take from the ground by mining. Minerals are the chemical compounds that make up rocks. Ore minerals are those which we can process into metals.

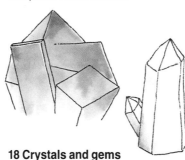

18 Crystals and gems

In many rocks, the minerals occur in the form of little glassy pieces we call crystals. Some crystals are very hard, very beautiful, and rare. We call them gems. Diamond is the finest gem of all.

19 Smelting

The main way of converting mineral ores into metals is smelting, which means heating them in a furnace with other materials. The most important smelting process is iron-smelting in a blast furnace.

20 Metals rule

Three-quarters of the chemical elements are metals, and most of them are used by people in one way or another. By far the most important is iron, followed by aluminium and copper. Iron is valued for its strength, aluminium for its lightness, and copper for its ability to conduct electricity well.

21 What a mix-up

Most metals are not used in the pure state. They are used instead in the form of a mixture, or alloy, with other metals or other elements. Our most useful metal, steel, is an alloy containing iron, a number of other metals, and traces of carbon.

22 Crude oil

After minerals, our most important raw material is petroleum, or crude oil. It is an organic material, the remains of tiny plants and animals that lived in the seas millions of years ago.

23 Chemicals from crude

Crude oil is a valuable raw material because it is made up of hundreds of different chemicals, called hydrocarbons. These chemicals are extracted at oil refineries, and are called petrochemicals.

24 Synthetics

The petrochemicals produced by processing oil are the starting point for a host of different materials that we use in the modern world. We call them synthetics. Among the best-known synthetics are plastics, synthetic fibres, dyes, pesticides, and drugs.

25 Plastics

Plastics are quite different from ordinary materials because of how they are made up. The molecules, or basic particles, of most materials are short. But the molecules of plastics are very long chains of carbon atoms.

GLOSSARY

(Note: Words in *italics* refer to other entries in the Glossary.)

Alloy A mixture of two or more *metals*, or of a metal and a non-metal (such as carbon).

Artificial elements *Elements* not found in nature that have been made by scientists. All are *radioactive*.

Asbestos A rock found in the form of fine fibres, used for insulation and for making fireproof suits.

Atoms The smallest particles of something that can exist.

Atom-smasher The popular name for a *particle accelerator*.

Bakelite The first *synthetic plastic*, named after the Belgian Leo Baekeland, who made it.

Blast furnace A furnace used to smelt *metals* such as iron and lead. It is so called because hot air is blasted into it to make it burn more fiercely.

Bronze An *alloy* of copper and tin. It was the first *metal* used on a large scale, about 3500 BC.

Casting A way of shaping *metal*, *plastic*, and glass, by pouring molten material into a mould, and allowing it to cool.

Cells The smallest units that make up the bodies of living things.

Celluloid The first *plastic*, made from cellulose, the woody substance in plants.

Cement A grey powder that forms the basis of *concrete*. It is made by roasting a mixture of limestone, clay, iron ore, and gypsum in a rotating kiln.

Ceramics Materials made by baking clay and other earthy materials in a kiln (oven). Pottery and *cement* are ceramic products.

Change of state A change of one *state of matter* into another – for example, a *liquid* into a *solid*.

Composite A *synthetic* material made of a *plastic*, and reinforced (strengthened) with a fibre, such as glass or carbon fibres.

Concrete One of our most useful materials of construction, made by mixing *cement* with sand, gravel or stone chips, and water. The wet concrete quickly sets stone-hard.

Condensation The change of state that occurs when a vapour (*gas*) is cooled and changes back into a *liquid*.

Cracking A chemical process that takes place in a *refinery*. Thick oils are broken down to give more useful products, such as petrol and chemicals.

Crust The hard outer layer of the Earth.

Crystals Natural forms of *minerals* that have a regular structure.

Die-casting A *manufacturing* process in which molten *metal* is cast into shape in a metal die (mould).

DNA The substance in a living *cell* that controls how it works and reproduces. DNA is short for deoxyribonucleic acid.

Electron A tiny particle found in all *atoms*. It has a negative electric charge.

Elements (chemical elements). The basic building blocks of matter. Over 90 are found in nature, and others have been made by scientists.

Evaporation The escape of molecules from a *liquid* to form a vapour (*gas*). It occurs at all temperatures, but fastest at the liquid's boiling point.

Fractionation The first main process in an oil *refinery*, in which crude oil is split up into a number of parts (fractions).

Gas One of the three *states of matter*. It has neither a fixed size nor a fixed shape.

Geode A hollow stone that is lined with *crystals*.

Geology The scientific study of the Earth.

Hardwoods Trees that yield hard timber, such as oak, beech, ebony, and mahogany.

Hydrocarbon A chemical containing hydrogen and carbon only. *Oil* is made up mainly of hydrocarbons.

Igneous rock One of the three main kinds of rock. It is formed when *magma* cools on or below the Earth's surface.

Liquid One of the three states of matter. It has a fixed size, but no fixed shape.

Machining Shaping *metals* by using power-driven machine tools, such as lathes and drills.

Magma Molten rock.

Margarine A *synthetic* food made mainly from plant oils and skimmed milk.

Mass production The manufacture of goods on a large scale.

Metal An *element* that is usually hard and shiny, and that conducts heat and electricity well. Most elements are metals.

Metamorphic rock One of the three main kinds of rock. It forms when existing rock re-melts.

Minerals The chemical materials that make up the rocks, and which we mine. Most *minerals* are composed of compounds of two or more *elements*.

Molecule The smallest particle of a substance. It contains two or more *atoms* joined together. A molecule often contains more than one different type of *atom*.

Neutron A particle found in the *nucleus* of every *atom* except hydrogen. It has no electric charge – it is neutral.

Nucleus The centre of an *atom*, made up mainly of two kinds of atomic particle, *protons* and *neutrons*. It is also the centre of a living *cell*, the part that contains the *DNA*.

Oil A liquid fuel extracted from the ground. It is properly called *petroleum*.

Open-cast mining Taking materials out of the ground from an open pit.

Ore A *mineral* from which a *metal* can be extracted.

Oxidation A chemical process in which substances combine with oxygen. Burning is an oxidation process that takes place in the air.

Particle accelerator A machine that accelerates subatomic particles and smashes them together. It is popularly called an *atom-smasher*.

Periodic table A method of arranging the elements in a table so as to bring out relationships between them.

Petrochemicals Chemicals obtained by processing *petroleum (oil)* in a *refinery*.

Petroleum The correct name for the *oil* we extract from the rocks. The word means 'rock oil'.

Pig iron The impure iron made in a *blast furnace*.

Planet One of nine large bodies that circle in space around the Sun. The Earth is a planet.

Plastic A *synthetic* product whose *molecules* take the form of long chains.

Plates Sections of the Earth's crust that 'float' on slowly-flowing soft rock underneath.

Proton A particle found in the *nucleus* of every *atom*. It has a positive electric charge.

Radiation Rays. The most common kind of radiation is electromagnetic radiation, which includes light rays and radio waves. *Radioactive* substances give off dangerous rays.

Radioactive elements A few natural *elements* that break down into different elements. As they break down, they give out dangerous *radiation*. All the *artificial elements* are radioactive.

Raw material A material that is the starting-point for making a product.

Refining Purifying materials, or turning them into more useful products.

Recycling Saving materials after they have been used once, and then using them again.

Refinery The chemical plant in which *oil* is split up and processed.

Robot In industry, a machine that is controlled by a computer, and carries out tasks that human workers once did.

Rusting A chemical process in which iron combines with the oxygen in the air to form rust.

Sedimentary rock One of the three main kinds of rock, made up from compressed layers of broken-down older rocks and fossils.

Smelting Heating *ores* in furnaces to extract the *metals* they contain.

Softwoods Trees that yield soft timber, such as pine and fir.

Solar System The family of bodies that travels through space together, centred on the Sun.

Solid One of the three *states of matter*. A solid has a fixed size and shape.

Star A huge globe of hot gas, which pours out energy mainly as heat and light.

States of matter The three forms in which matter is found on Earth – *solid, liquid,* and *gas*.

Steel Our most important *metal*. It is an *alloy*, consisting mainly of iron, together with traces of manganese and other metals, and a little carbon.

Surface tension Forces acting at the surface of a liquid that make the liquid behave as if it had a kind of 'skin'.

Synthetics Materials that are made completely from chemicals.

Universe All that exists. The Universe contains the materials around us, and all matter – the Earth, the Sun, the stars, the galaxies and even space itself.

Uranium A *radioactive element* found in nature. It forms the fuel used in most nuclear reactors.

Volcano An opening in the Earth's crust through which molten rock, ash, and fumes escape.

Water cycle The natural process by which water continually circulates between the Earth's surface and the air.

Welding A method of joining *metals* by heating, or melting the parts in contact.

Wood-pulp The raw material from which paper and some *plastics* are made. The wood is broken down into a mass of fibres.

INDEX

(Page numbers in *italics* refer to the illustrations and captions.)